T0196937

prayer**think**

a collection of prayers
for all people

roy k. bohrer

PRAYERTHINK
A COLLECTION OF PRAYERS FOR ALL PEOPLE

New International Version (NIV)
Holy Bible, New International Version®, NIV® Copyright ©1973, 1978, 1984, 2011 by Biblica, Inc.® Used by permission. All rights reserved worldwide.

King James Version (KJV)
Public Domain

Common English Bible (CEB)
Copyright © 2011 by Common English Bible

iUniverse books may be ordered through booksellers or by contacting:

iUniverse
1663 Liberty Drive
Bloomington, IN 47403
www.iuniverse.com
1-800-Authors (1-800-288-4677)

ISBN: 978-1-5320-5427-3 (sc)
ISBN: 978-1-5320-5426-6 (e)

Library of Congress Control Number: 2018955335

Print information available on the last page.

iUniverse rev. date: 08/21/2018

Praying For All People

"I urge, then, first of all, that petitions, PRAYERS, intercession and thanksgiving be made FOR ALL PEOPLE — that we may live peaceful and quiet lives in all godliness and holiness." I *Timothy 2:1-2 (NIV)*

"Moreover, as for me, God forbid that I should sin against the Lord in ceasing to pray for you." *1 Samuel 12:23 (KJV)*

"I have no desire but to do all men good. I feel to pray for all men." *Joseph Smith, History of the Church of Jesus Christ of Latter-day Saints, 7 Vols. 5:259*

"Our earnest prayer is that God will graciously vouchsafe prosperity, happiness, and peace to all our neighbors, and like blessings to all the peoples and powers of the earth." *U.S. President William McKinley*

"When my arms can't reach people who are close to my heart, I always hug them with my prayers." *Hussein Nishah*

Contents

MY FAMILY

SPECIAL RELATIONSHIPS

THOSE I SEE DAILY

THOSE FOR WHOM I DO NOT WANT TO PRAY, BUT I WILL

STRANGERS

THOSE WHO SERVE ME

MEDICAL CARETAKERS

PEOPLE IN VARIOUS CIRCUMSTANCES

ENTERTAINERS AND BROADCASTERS

PEOPLE IN FOREIGN LANDS

A PRAYER FOR YOU

Dedication

This book is dedicated to my parents, teachers, and friends who led me to have consideration for all people.

Learning Prayerthink

Have you ever prayed so intently for someone that it became the focus of your day and your time? Think of doing that for many people in a day. That is the idea of prayerthink. I have a master's degree in theology, and I was a pastor for many years, but the simple basic premise of this book is that prayer works – for the one receiving prayer and for the one doing the praying.

I prayed for a job, and a job opened up. I prayed for safety, and safety came. I prayed for resolution of a problem, and it was resolved. Throughout the years I prayed aloud with and for many people, but I also prayed thousands of prayers that no other person ever heard. I still do.

Having prayer for others as a large part of our daily thought process is prayerthink.

I invite you to get up in the morning and determine to pray for all with whom you will speak that day – or all you will see – or all the family members and acquaintances of whom you can think. You will usually then find you have no energy or time for self-pity or loneliness.

Instead of snubbing or cursing people who hurt you, holding a grudge, or becoming upset and sad, pray for those persons. Ask a blessing for them, ask divine help and guidance for them. Commit them to divine care, and commit yourself to a spiritual viewpoint. Do not let your day or your life be ruined by negativity, unnecessary pain (often unintentional) or disappointment.

You will be a happier person! You will be a godlier person. We are in this world at this time with many, many people, and we were not meant to live alone. In ways that go beyond our understanding, we complete our own lives in a satisfying way by our involvement with others. Religious writings emphasize the importance of considering others with compassion and love.... even the stranger....even the enemy. One of the most loving things you can do, especially if you cannot do any physical action for people, is to hold them up in prayer for the blessings and presence of the almighty.

ASAP – Always Say A Prayer!

This book is just a beginning; it is a sampler collection of prayers for all people. It is not meant to be read in sequence cover to cover, but it is to be a reference book of examples of prayers you may wish to use as people and circumstances arise. The prayers here for so many different people suggest that you think about all of the people you encounter, in any way, perhaps many about whom you would never usually think. Let your thoughts flow into prayers for those persons, asking that they may be helped and their lives may be edified. A prayer does not need to be many words. No words need to be spoken aloud; the prayers are said in your mind and heart; they are the way you think as you walk through life. (Jesus suggested in Matthew 6:6 (CEB) "When you pray, go to your room, shut the door, and pray to your Father who is present in that secret place. Your Father who sees what you do in secret will reward you.") People need never know what you are doing, or if it seems helpful to some you know, you may sometimes tell them, "I prayed for you today."

In addition to invoking divine intervention and blessing upon many people, some of whom may not have any other prayers offered for them, you are bringing the power of God and good into the whole world.

Praying for all people takes the selfishness and worry about yourself out of your life. This is why you will be happier and you will feel more like an integral and important part of the world. We live in such a tense, controversial, biting, stabbing time. Praying people of God can do something about it. You will be fulfilling a divine mission.

NOTE: There is white space on the prayer pages to encourage you to write your thoughts, notes, memories or intentions about people for whom you prayed. You can make this book a personal prayer diary.

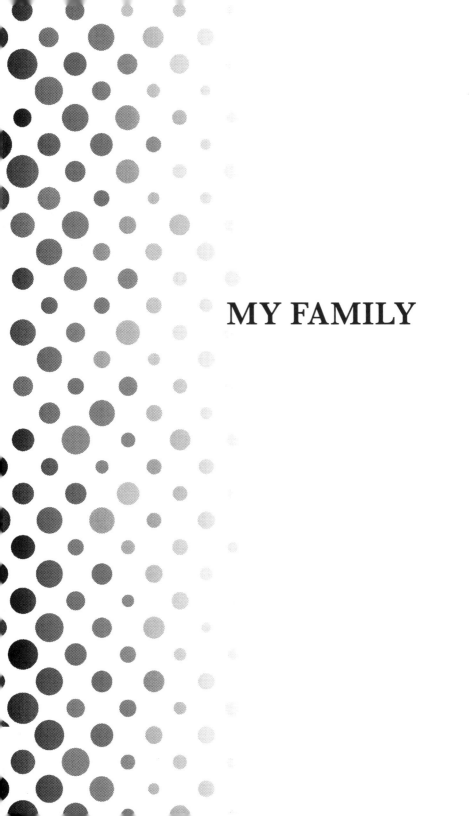

MY FAMILY

Mother

I have no idea how often my mother has prayed for me, but I am praying for her, Lord, with thanks that you gave her to me. Thank you for all that my mother has meant to me and all she has done for me. Bless her with satisfaction and joy in her role as a mother, and in her life generally. Mothers seem to be among the most self-giving people, but I pray that my mother can also receive some good things that are meaningful to her. Help me to give to her, Lord, as she has given so much. Forgive her, Lord, for the mistakes she has made, whether or not they are known to her, as I know she is not perfect. If it is your will, grant her many years of life, with good health and happy days. Give her the desires of her heart that are good for her. Hold her close to you, Lord, and give her a strong faith. Amen

Father

God, you are called father by many different peoples, because a father's loving care is an example of your loving care. Thank you for my father, for all that he has done for me through the years, and for the love he has given me, whether or not he expressed it, because we know that fathers often are not good at expressing love. Give my father a strength in living that he may be upheld in all things. Grant him satisfaction in his life, his work, and his role as a father. We know he is not perfect, so bless him with an understanding and acceptance of forgiveness, grace and mercy. Help him to trust in you with a strong faith and to confidently place his life in your hands. According to your will, give him a long and healthy life with a feeling of security in all things. Amen

Sisters and Brothers

I ask you to bless my sister(s) or brother(s) with a good life, strengthened with love in many places, self-confidence, and divine faith in all things. They are a part of me, my siblings, and that is a gift from you, O Lord. Sometimes I feel close to them and sometimes I do not, but regardless of my feelings, Lord, I pray that you will stay close to them in all of their needs and in all circumstances. May we be friends throughout our lifetimes. Give them joy in our family, in their own families, and in their relationships with others. Grant them success in their endeavors so they will have good things and good times to celebrate. May they always have enough of what they need, and may they have healthy lives. I commend them into your care. Amen

Grandparents

I am glad to be able to enjoy grandparents, Lord, because many people do not have those blessings, or at least they do not have them for very long. Let my grandparents feel that they are blessings and are loved, even with the needs and changes of older age. They are important as the parents of my parents and my aunts and uncles. Help me to do whatever I can to be loving and helpful to them. Health, security, satisfaction, stability are all needs they have; please bless them with these gifts and many other things that are good for them. May they always have enough to fulfill their needs. May their numerous years and their maturity provide them with good decisions and rewarding days. Most of all, Lord, keep them strong in faith for whatever they must face. Give them the assurance of your love and grace. Walk closely with them until the end. Amen

Aunts and Uncles

The siblings of my parents, my aunts and uncles, probably carried me when I was a baby and cared for me and helped me as I was growing up. They are quite diverse in personalities and ways of life, but they all need your grace, mercy and love, Lord. Some are closer to me than others in various ways, but I want to ask that you work in all of their lives so that they may have peace, love, success and satisfaction. Take care of them as they have helped to take care of me and other family members; they have often been like angels in disguise. Give them joy in their work and in their families. Give them spiritual faith to sustain them. Let them get along well with each other and with all of the family, so that they may know blessings from our life together. Especially as they advance in years, I pray that you will help them, Lord, in all times of grief and trouble, so that may know strength and courage to meet whatever comes to them. Keep them in your love. Amen

Crazy Guy

Lord, please protect him from his own craziness. Amen

Cousins

Someone once said that cousins are usually your first friends, your closest friends, and that seems to be true with some of mine. I thank you, Lord, for my cousins, those I know well and those I hardly know at all, because they are all part of my family. Thank you for the help, advice and friendship from my cousins. Give to each one of them a satisfying and happy life that comes from spiritual faith and good usage of their own gifts. Bless them in whatever special needs they may have. Within their own individual families may they be blessed with understanding, acceptance, and joy. May they have their daily needs met, and even more to enjoy and share with others. When they need help in the difficult times, times of sadness and trouble and confusion, please uplift and sustain them. Help us to stick together. Let us live in family love and encouragement. Amen

Spouse or Partner

You have given me great joy in my spouse or partner, Lord, and I am so thankful for that gift of another life that walks with me. Let that special person be enriched by me and my love, even as I am enriched by our relationship. Give to my loved one whatever is needed in daily life to bring a good feeling of security, satisfaction, peacefulness and love. In the times of worry and trouble, bring sustaining faith, along with answers that are needed. When we are having a disagreement or conflict, Lord, help us both to be understanding, patient, and forgiving. Let our lives be intertwined for strength and growth, not for burden or guilt. Help us to share life in such a way that we may both be lifted up and our loads may be lightened. Keep my special partner in my love and in your care and faith forever. Amen

Child

You gave me the life of my child, Lord, and the best thing I can do is to keep committing that life into your care. That is my prayer today and every day, whether I say it or not; take care of my child in your protecting, nourishing love. You know better than any of us what needs, gifts, desires and circumstances my child has, so bless that dear child of mine according to your will. My desire and hope, Lord, is that my child will have a life full of peace, satisfaction, success, joy and fulfillment, topped off with a spiritual faith in your grace and love – this is my constant prayer. Bring health and healing for every attack. Bring forgiveness for all mistakes. Bring friends and loving relationships. Give my child a long and meaningful life here and an eternal life with you. Amen

Grandchild

My grandchild is special, one who is not under my immediate care but nevertheless one for whom I have a great love and life interest, so I pray for your wonderful blessings to be showered upon my grandchild. I pray that this loved one will know the joy of feeling special but will not let that position detract from a life of responsibility and goodness and love to others. Please give my grandchild good health, good thinking, and good relationships with parents, family and many others through the years. Lead, O Lord, to a successful and productive life that will bring all necessities and many joys. Help my grandchild to use talents, gifts and opportunities for good. Keep this beloved one in a spiritual faith that will constantly give guidance, reassurance, grace, comfort, and hope for all of this life and that to come. Amen

Family Member Who Does Not Speak To Me

Life brings with it the effects of evil, often unexpected, like the situation that has come between me and the family member who is not speaking to me. It does not really matter much who is to blame, and I am not sure that I even understand what has happened. I am saddened, Lord, and I beg your forgiveness for whatever evil and error I have committed to cause this. Help me to find the opportunity to express my apology and sadness to this family member who is offended. The injunction to pray for your enemies comes to my mind, so Lord, I am asking you to bless this person with understanding, forgiveness, mercy, love, strength and whatever else may be needed to diffuse the anger and coldness that has ensued. Help both of us to see that not speaking is not a helpful loving family attitude, and we should both act to resolve it. None of us is perfect; we all need mercy and forgiveness daily, so help us to embrace this faith. We may not even like each other very much, but let us put godly love into practice. Amen

Distant Relatives

Lord, I pray for distant relatives who are part of my family, many whom I do not often see and hardly know. The needs of all people are much the same, however, so I ask you to grant to them peace and satisfaction in their lives, protection and health in their days, optimism and joy in their attitudes, love and success in their relationships. Where they have troubles and heartaches, uplift them and give them strength. Grant to them the desires of their hearts, according to your will. Give them a spiritual faith that will keep them close to you throughout their days and years, so that they may walk with you all the way. Amen

Disturbed Girl

Lord, let your Spirit overtake her spirit. Amen

In-laws

My in-laws have become my family through marriage, so I have a love and concern for them as for my own blood relatives. As I think about my various in-laws, I ask you, Lord, to be with them always, giving them protection, care and happiness in life. Go with them where they must go, and enable them for what they must do. When there is a special need, a threat, a danger or loss, uplift them and keep them strong, patient and steadfast. Bless them with a spiritual faith that will enrich their days and strengthen their lives throughout the years. Keep us united in concern, attitude and communication since we share life through our loved ones. Amen

Pet

My pet is like family, a gift to me to be a part of my life. Pets are part of your creation, Lord, and I ask you to bless and protect my companion that I enjoy. Because I cannot communicate with the pet as well as with people, I do not always understand my pet's circumstances and needs, but I know that you do, Lord, so I place it into your care. Help me to take good care of this pet, that I may have the companionship for a long time. Whatever animals might know or feel or want, bless this pet with good things for its life. Protect it from sickness and harm. Let this pet enjoy life with me, as my life is enriched by it. Amen

Me

Keep me going, Lord, for as long as I have time in this world.

Keep me loving as much as I can.

Keep me humble, to see my flaws and to admit them.

Keep me strong in faith.

Keep me from evils and despairs that burden me.

Keep me optimistic about all that is good and godly.

Keep me interested in all people.

Keep me praying for all people.

Keep me filled with joy for life.

Keep me going, Lord, for as long as I have time in this world.

Keep me, Lord. Amen

SPECIAL
RELATIONSHIPS

Close Friends

You can't choose your family, but you can choose your friends. Thank you, Lord, that you have helped me to choose some close friends in my life. Bless my friends with the knowledge that they are special and important to me, that they may have the satisfaction of being loving helpers for me. As our lives have turned out, my close friends and I have shared much and cared for each other a great deal, and this could only have come because you guided us. Be with my close friends, Lord, so that they may have a loving assurance and strength to help them in their daily lives. Give them protection, good health and everything needed to sustain them, even as they have helped to sustain me. My friends should be blessed with love, satisfaction, happiness and spiritual faith. Keep us close together, Lord, and keep my friends enriched with good things from your hand to uplift them, especially when they are having times of trouble and weakness. May my close friends and I rest in your care. Amen

Disappointed, Lost Love, Lost Life

Heal our hearts, O Lord, heal our hearts. Amen

Any Friend

Thank you, Lord, that my life has brought to me friendships from various places, so that I may know the closeness of relationships and the meaning of interest and love from other people. I am thinking about one of my friends now, and asking your blessing on this life that is dear to me. I know some of the special needs of this friend, but not all of them, so I ask your good gifts and help for whatever this friend needs in life, even those things that my friend does not realize. Let me be a helper, an adviser, a listener, a caretaker, a communicator, a goer, a doer, whatever may be needed. Let my friend be uplifted when extra strength is needed. Let my friend know acceptance and love when reassurance is needed. Let my friend be sustained by spiritual faith in all circumstances. Let my friend know peace, love, and satisfaction. Amen

A Good Man

He is trying so hard, Lord; help him to fulfill his goals. Amen

A Lover

I pray for the special person with whom I now enjoy a loving relationship, as two persons who have grown close in love and life. Be with this person who is investing time and interest in me that there may be a satisfying good feeling through the days, weeks and years of our time. Meet the needs, lift the burdens, heal the weaknesses, solve the problems, forgive the wrongs, ease the strains, increase the patience, guide the decisions, dispel the doubts, increase the joys, O Lord.

Make us good for each other. We do not know how our relationship will endure, what the goal may be, or what the ties of love might mean, but continue to guide and strengthen both of us, Lord, that we may walk forward with your help and blessing. Amen

Someone Who Is like Family

I am blessed, Lord, by having persons in my life that are close and loving, who feel like family, as they say. Let your loving presence and ongoing help bless this person who did not come into my life as family, but who certainly has a place of love and concern and closeness like a family member. Let this dear person feel the rewards and satisfaction of interest and loyalty that have come to us. When there is a special circumstance or a special need, Lord, be there with your strengthening power. Where there is a weakness or problem, be there with your leading and healing. I care about this person, Lord, and I ask that your love and grace will be important and meaningful in this life. Sustain my friend with spiritual faith, as well as the love of our relationship. Amen

Divorced Spouse

We learn forgiveness, acceptance and renewal from your love, O Lord, so I ask for those blessings in the life of my former spouse. Whatever happened, whatever changed, whatever one or the other did, let us both be beyond finger-pointing, accusations, embarrassment, hostility, grudges, guilt or grief, as we accept change of relationship, mercy and forgiveness. Give my former spouse a positive attitude toward the future, a realistic acceptance of what has happened, and a sense of renewal in life. Grant continuing satisfaction, love and joy, according to your great merciful love for us. Help us to think and relate as people who do not have the same marriage bond we once had, but who still have a bond of concern for each other. Let us strive for peacefulness. Amen

THOSE I SEE DAILY

Neighbors

I didn't choose my neighbors, but they are near to me every day, Lord, as you have placed us to live close to each other. Give them help in their living, that they may be sustained in their families, jobs, relationships and needs. I do not know a great deal about them, but I do know they have the same needs as all people, to live peacefully and successfully in this world. Whatever their needs may be, whatever their problems may be, whatever their desires and goals may be, grant to my neighbors a faith that will keep them going. If they do not know spiritual faith, work in their hearts and lives, Lord, that they may gain a faith. Since we live closely, let me be instrumental in their lives to help them in whatever ways I can. Amen

Someone with Whom I Work

I am thinking about a person with whom I work and the needs of that person. You know the lives and hearts of all people, Lord, so I ask your blessing for this fellow worker who has needs that I really do not know. I see this person and communicate daily, so I know many things; I know there is a need for joy and satisfaction in life, for happy relationships and peaceful family, for strength in trials and guidance in decisions, and for spiritual faith. Grant all of these, Lord, and beyond these, give this person whatever else is necessary for good living. In instances where corrections have to be made, problems have to be endured, and flaws have to be healed, grant your unlimited grace, Lord. Sustain this fellow worker with your everlasting love and mercy. Amen

My Supervisor or Boss

My boss doesn't have an easy job and is just another human being, like all of us who work together. Help all of us to remember this truth with an attitude of acceptance and a willingness to cooperate. Sustain my boss in the job that has to be done, with all the conflicts that arise and all the feelings that are involved. Give my boss gifts of understanding and patience in dealing with me, as well as with other people and situations. Give also the gifts of leadership, fairness, administration, organization and faithfulness to the task. When failures threaten, tempers flare, or the pressures come from higher up, give my boss stability, insight and wisdom. There is a place for faith, bringing mercy and love in my boss's life, so grant these blessings as well. Amen

Store Personnel

As I shop in my favorite stores, I notice the personnel who work to keep the store open, some of whom I know, some of whom are strangers to me. Thinking about the store clerk today, grant to this person the patience, insight and acceptance to be able to serve customers in a helpful and pleasant way. There is a big variety of customers, so the job is not easy; therefore I ask you, Lord, to steady this clerk with guidance and perseverance. Thinking about the person I saw stocking shelves, there is another job that can make a person feel very thankless and unappreciated. Give this person a feeling of satisfaction in the job and importance in the overall picture of service. Bring to the store personnel an appreciation for their jobs and a happiness in doing their service. Let me be one who shows them appreciation and concern instead of trouble. Amen

A Nice Lady

Help her to become even better and to enjoy her satisfaction. Amen

Others at the Gym

All the people working out at the fitness gym I attend, from young to old, are trying to improve their lives and health. My mind and prayer are centered now on those I just saw there, and I am asking for your sustaining power to give them the willpower and energy to do the exercises that will help them and keep them in good shape. In some cases, Lord, there is a disease or condition that needs healing; please give your healing power. In some cases there are adjustments that need to be made in strength, ability, weight, flexibility, or attitude; grant your blessing to their efforts. In all cases there needs to be a desire for improvement and a determination to keep trying; give them the right motivations and attitudes, Lord. Life is not complete without a spiritual faith, so grant to them that blessing also for their good. Amen

Fellow Volunteers

Volunteers are doing a service for good for many different reasons. Bless those who do volunteer service with me, Lord, that they may have a feeling of reward and joy in their tasks. They are not serving for reward, but grant to them a spirit of dedication and joy that will uplift them and enrich their lives. Keep them focused on the importance of what they are doing and the good they are achieving as they do their service. Give them positive attitudes toward the people being helped and the tasks being done, even though these volunteers are not being compensated. Help all of us to have a spirit of cooperation, acceptance and understanding as we work together for the good of our cause. Amen

People Who Work in My Building

I see the same people in my work building every day, Lord, and even though I do not know them very well, I want to reach out to them in prayer to support their lives. We have a connection, a bond, just by being placed close to each other daily in the work setting. Because of that bond, I ask you, Lord, to work in their lives to grant these people their necessities and the important mercies that will bring contentment and joy to life. Give them satisfaction in their work, no matter what skill level it may be. Personally bring to these people good health, safety, loving relationships, positive attitudes, and a spiritual faith that will sustain them in all days and years of life. Amen

THOSE FOR WHOM I DO NOT WANT TO PRAY, BUT I WILL

Someone I Don't Like

In spiritual laws and parental training, we are told to love everyone and be good to all. For the majority of people I meet, this is not difficult, but I am thinking about one person now who I just do not like. This person has ways of acting and speaking that I do not agree with and in my opinion has very wrong motives and attitudes. Let your presence and power strengthen this person, Lord. May your forgiving love be a force for good in me and in the life of this person. No one should be unlikeable. I can be accepting, and even good to this person. It is not important that I like everyone, but I pray that there can be a peacefulness, warmth and likeable nature in both of us so that there can be positive life experiences between us. Give a spiritual blessing, Lord, so that your will and your ways are also considered by this other person. Help me not to offend this person. Amen

One Who Stole from Me

Possessions are just things, but when someone wrongly takes my things, it is an offense to me, a disappointment and a loss, not only of the things, but of respect for the ones who steal. Please work in the hearts of those who have stolen to make them humble, to see and admit errors, and to change their personalities. Call up in the hearts of those who have stolen a feeling of guilt, a sincere repentance, and a desire to do justice. Lord, I am not as concerned about my loss of things as I am for the human heart that accepted the evil of stealing as an acceptable way of life. Let me be forgiving, and also help these persons to learn and change. Amen

Person Who Tried to Hurt My Feelings

I am aware that a person has tried to hurt my feelings, causing me grief and sadness and negativity. I don't want to feel hurt, Lord, and also I do not want to feel ill will about this person. I do not understand the reasons or the motives behind this attempt to hurt me, but I know it is not fair or good. Work in the heart of this person, Lord, to bring words and actions to full light and understanding. If there is denial or unacceptance, let the truth come out and prevail. My prayer, Lord, is that this person may have a change of heart and a change of attitude, that there may not be harm produced, but rather helpfulness, love and peace. Let my hurts be healed, and let the relationship between me and this person also be healed. Amen

Unfriendly Clerk

I feel angry and mistreated when, as a customer of a store or business, I am ignored, misinformed, or mistreated. I pray for the clerk that I encountered who, in my opinion, is not doing an acceptable job. Other customers and I are being offended by unresponsiveness, inability, lack of concern, or impoliteness, and I am not sure if this clerk has been trained, has the proper personality for the job, or is even aware of the offensiveness. Please intercede in a merciful and powerful way, Lord, so that this person can get some help and can change for good. Whatever it may take, whoever can assume responsibility, Lord, may your concern and love be present in order to correct a sad situation. People do not generally want to be bad. Let some goodness prevail to help this clerk. Amen

One Who Offended Me

I have considered my own feelings and the circumstances by which I was offended, and it is difficult to sort out where the most guilt may rest. I do not like to feel offended and I do not like barriers between people, so I am asking your help, Lord, to bring this offense to a close in my mind and, if necessary, also in the other person. Lead me to forgiveness, understanding, acceptance, and overlooking. Lead me to be a person of peacefulness and joy. I am forgiving the person who caused my feelings of offense, and help me to do whatever may be necessary for healing in the other person as well. I am letting go of the offense and will not let it stand in the way of any relationship. Help me to always go forward, Lord, not backward or holding on to a grudge. Amen

Certain National Figures

Some well-known people in the world are very unlikeable to me, Lord, for a variety of reasons. They are your creation also, and I pray that they will serve your purposes, whether they know it or not. I think some are making too much money, some have too much power, some are not good influences for children, youth or anyone, but who am I to judge what assets or influences others have been given? I pray for your influence in their lives, Lord, so they may seek your truth and your will. No one is beyond the realm of your influence and your power, so use them for good. It doesn't matter whether I or anyone else likes these high-profile national figures; what matters is that they are committed in prayer to your care, your love, your mercy and your power. That is what I am doing. Help me to remember that. Amen

Certain Government Officials

In our world, people are supportive of different political parties and philosophies, and generally we think the variety and the challenges are good. I am not so sure what is for the good these days, but it is inevitable that I will not agree with the politics and decisions of our leaders that are not in sympathy with my views. I commend our government officials into your care and keeping, Lord, even those with whom I disagree. Work in and through all of our officials so that, together, they may serve you and your purposes for the nation and the world. These officials have secular earthly powers, Lord, in their elected or appointed positions, so use them for good and for godliness. You have allowed governments to stand, Lord, so help me to accept them and do whatever I can to be of help to them, including those that are not of my persuasion. Amen

Someone I Cannot Understand

Misunderstanding can cause a great deal of hardship and heartbreak, so I pray for help in understanding someone whom I definitely cannot seem to understand. My mind can be closed, unaccepting, and selfish. I pray for your power and love to open up any blockages I have with this person. The other person may have a problem with me that is hampering our communication. I pray for your power and love to help our mutual understanding. Differences in backgrounds, attitudes and outlooks can make understanding difficult, but it is not impossible to learn, to be more open, to be accepting. Please give me these blessings, Lord, especially to help with this particular person. Amen

One Who Always Disagrees

It seems odd that I find agreement with most persons, but there is this one with whom I always seem to be in disagreement. Maybe we have a conflict of personality, a barrier that has risen, or we are just so very different. I am uncomfortable with always being in disagreement with this person, and I seek your help, Lord, in coming to some better communicating or relating. Perhaps it cannot change, and that may not necessarily be bad, but show me some things, move me, help me to make sure I am accepting, allow us to be friendly with each other. Even though disagreements are not necessarily bad, when it is constant, it is not pleasant. Open up insight and understanding for me in this situation, Lord. Amen

Someone I Could Hate

Of course we all like some people more than others, we get along better with some than others, and we enjoy some persons more than others. But I know that hatred is wrong, and I need your love and mercy mightily flowing in and through me to help me not to hate a person. This is one of your created persons for something, although I do not know what. Keep me from hatred, Lord; let me see something differently. Let me be forgiving, let me understand, let me adjust, let me be more sympathetic, let love be more powerful than hate. Also, please work in this other person with your love and mercy to keep faith, goodness and godliness in view. The power to change comes from your love, Lord. Amen

My Enemies

One of the hardest injunctions from your word, Lord, is to love our enemies. There are those personal enemies who, I believe, have harmed me or want to harm me. There are enemies of loved ones who want to hurt them, enemies of my nation who have warred against us or will war against us, and enemies of my church who seek to destroy it. I cannot agree with their ungodliness, nor their evil acts and desires, whoever they are, and I am certain that you, O Lord, would have us to recognize evil and reject it. But your admonition is that we love them as fellow creations, joint inhabitants of the world, people who share the same blessings, and people who have been redeemed in your love. I pray for their acceptance of your love and grace, that evil may not win the victory in them. I pray for the indwelling and work of your Spirit in them for change and for good. Protect me from the victories of evil and cover me with your power and love. Amen

STRANGERS

Lady Begging on the Street

I know that this lady I saw today begging does not want to look like she does and does not want to be doing what she is doing. Lord, I feel so sorry for her. Grant her some assurance that she is your child, O God, and that when all earthly love and help seem far away, you will not forsake her. Give this lady a spiritual faith that will help to override her physical needs. In whatever ways she can be helped, Lord, please help her to eat and rest and survive. Take care of this poor lady, Lord. Amen.

Person Driving the Car In Front of Me

Maybe the person driving in front of me is happy, maybe not. Maybe that person is healthy, maybe not. Maybe that person is relaxed, maybe not. I pray for the person driving in front of me, not knowing anything about him or her, but knowing that one has a need for you in life, Lord, and a need for a life of satisfaction and health. Whatever that person needs, O Lord, please give it to him or her according to your will and desires. Whatever might be wrong, Lord, help it to get fixed. Bring spiritual faith in a meaningful way. Keep that driver safe, reaching whatever destination and whatever fulfillment is right and good. Keep that person focused on the right and good all the time. Amen

Homeless Persons under the Bridge

I pray for the persons I saw living under a bridge, Lord; surely you know them, whether or not they acknowledge you. I don't think anyone really wants to live under a bridge, but circumstances have brought them to this existence. Lift them up, Lord, so they can see some measure of satisfaction and care in their lives. Lift them up, Lord, to a spiritual faith that will sustain them and heal them. Lift them up, Lord, so that they know love. Keep them warm physically and spiritually and socially, that their lives may be sustained. Keep them in your care, Lord. Amen

Someone Shopping in Store

I am bringing to you in prayer, Lord, that person that caught my attention while I was shopping in the store. Whoever she is, I know that she needs your power and your strength. She needs to know your love, Lord, and to enjoy love in her life. Whether she has a lot of this world's goods or very little, she deserves to have a satisfaction and joy in her life. Grant to her the desires of her heart, Lord, if they are good for her. Keep her life focused on the most important things: spiritual faith, love, health and peacefulness. Give her joy in her family and relationships. Give her joy in her shopping, that she may feel satisfied with what she has. Amen

Those for Whom I Am Concerned

Help him, Lord, guide him, lead him. Amen

Help her, Lord, guide her, lead her. Amen

Teenager I Saw

When I see a teenager like I saw today, Lord, all I can think of and wish for is stability and success and joy for the future. A teenager is emerging, finding, developing, with so much future ahead. Bless that teenager with these most needful things, Lord, and help that person grow into full maturity as a successful, independent, healthy adult. And most important, keep that teen in a spiritual faith all along the way, that your will might be sought and your love might be cherished. Give that teenager a full measure of your protection and love now and through the years ahead. Amen

Cute Little Baby
with Its Parent

To see a baby with its parent is an inspiration for all of us, Lord, an indication of the future and your ongoing promises in the world. Especially bless that baby and parent I saw today, as they need your guidance, strength and mercy. Give them a knowledge of your love that will keep them close to you. The parent needs help in the important job of caretaker, educator and motivator. The baby needs help in healthy development, growth, and protection. Grant to them their basic needs, Lord, and beyond that, the special blessings that will make them special persons. Amen

Person on the Elevator

Every person has joys and sorrows, problems and successes, ups and downs, Lord, like the person on the elevator with me. I know nothing specific about this person, but I am praying that you will grant the knowledge of your grace, mercy and love to this person, to uphold and sustain that life that you want to bless. I don't know what is especially needed or wanted, but I do know that everyone wants to be loved, to be sustained, and to be a success in some way. Bless this person with these things I pray, O Lord. Keep your guiding hands and everlasting love close. Amen

Little Boy in the Store

The interest and enthusiasm of the little boy I saw is heartwarming and encouraging. To see such a little one pick up an item, examine it, feel it, carry it, and show it to others reminds me of how blessed all of us are in our life experiences; the blessings start young and they go on. Give this little boy a joy in living and experiencing through his years. Give him other people in his life that will allow him to experience, that will guide him well, and share his enthusiasm for your good blessings. Give him parents, teachers and caregivers who will notice his talents and interests and help to mold him as the unique individual that he is. Lord, may he grow up to be a happy and successful man who will know love in many ways and will know faith in you. May he never lose his interest and enthusiasm for life. May he have a knowledge of the things of God, a healthy reverence for life, and a lasting commitment to spiritual faith. Amen

Young Couple in the Park

The young man and the young woman seem so much in love, dancing, caressing, and kissing. Lord, give them blessings in their loving relationship. Let them experience the goodness of your world through their love and interest in each other. Whether they are a new couple or have been together for a long time, guide them in their affection and actions so that they can be self-giving rather than selfish. Bring good out of their interest in each other, and do not let them be harmed by their sharing of life and love. They probably have many years yet to live, with each other or not, so give to each of them a satisfaction and appreciation of life that will provide peace and joy throughout the years. Give them a faith in you, Lord, so they can know that all love is a reflection of your great love for people, and all goodness comes from your hand of blessing. Amen

People Waiting with Me in Medical Office

Everyone sitting in the medical office is here for some problem, some treatment, some help. Grant your comfort and peace, Lord, to this one I see waiting with me. According to your will, grant your healing power so that the medical treatments might be successful. Give a spiritual faith to this person that your everlasting mercy and love might be believed and felt. Since medical concerns are usually fears, grant your comfort and reassurance to this person, so that he or she may not be without hope. I commend this person into your care, O Lord. Amen

Someone I Saw at a Meeting or Gathering

Grant your blessing, Lord, to the person I saw at the meeting. It is difficult to know the special needs of this person, but whatever they are, grant a full measure of your merciful support and assistance. There are problems that need attention. There are needs to be filled. There are mistakes to be forgiven. There is love to be nourished. There are tasks to be completed. Grant to this person the skills and interests that are necessary, and the faith to endure and move forward. Give to this person a joy in living and a healthy attitude for each day. Amen

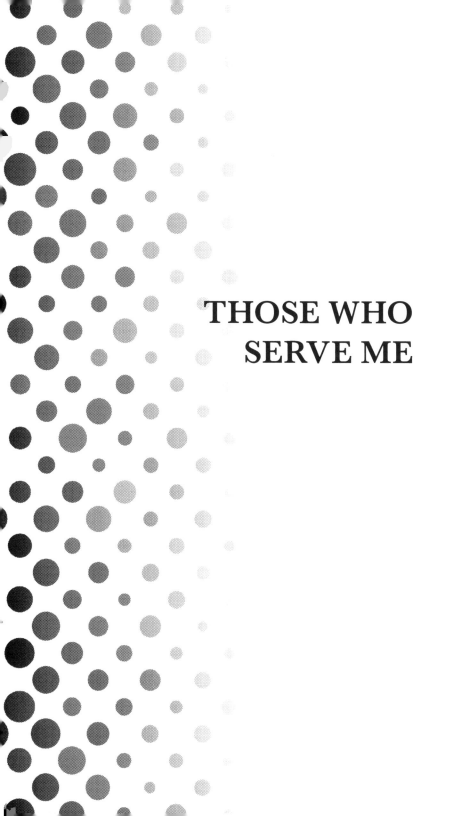

THOSE WHO
SERVE ME

Farmers and Producers Who Made My Food

I do not usually think about who has had a part in making my soup, my sandwich or my ice cream, but thank you, Lord, for those who have planted, grown, developed, harvested, processed, canned, packaged, sold and delivered my foods. How much we take in without any thought for those who have provided their services! Bless these providers with health, protection, satisfaction and good returns for their labors. I fear that many are working with almost no return; take care of them, Lord, that they will have enough and will have positive lives. Those who provide our foods, which we often have in abundance, are so important to our lives; Lord, bless their lives with the desires of their hearts and the joy of serving your people and your world. Amen

Those Who Produced My Clothing

Thanks to the people who have labored to provide my clothing, from beginning to end, the product in my hands. Grant a joy and satisfaction to them in the labors and production they are doing for the final usage and pleasure of so many, like myself, who receive the results of their efforts, clothing to wear and enjoy. Give to them a sense of accomplishment in knowing how much pleasure their products are bringing to wearers everywhere. Clothes make the man is an old adage that has much truth in it because of the attitudes of wearers and viewers, so these industry people serve a very important role, which I pray they will know. Amen

Police Officers

The protection and regulation of our society lies in police officers who often serve thanklessly and in danger. Lord, give to police officers protection in their duties and a pride of accomplishment in their work. Grant that those who voluntarily accept the responsibilities of a job that is so necessary and important to our society may receive not only physical compensation but also the mental satisfaction of knowing the importance of their service. Grant to them and to their families a peacefulness of knowing that they serve you and your people in their important work. Grant them your guiding hand and love throughout their days. Amen

Firefighters

Those who strive to protect and save lives and property from the danger of fire are not only to be thanked for their service, but blessed by God for taking such an important job. Lord, grant to firefighters the fruits of their labors, protection and guidance in their tasks, and a feeling of accomplishment in their service. Protect them in their duties as they protect others. Save them as they save others. Give them wisdom and insight in their work as they seek to serve your people and your world, Lord. Bless them and their families with your loving care. Amen

U. S. Military Forces

Our military personnel serve in many places and in many capacities for our citizens and our country. The people of our nation owe them a debt of gratitude for their service. Lord, I ask you to grant protection to every one of our military personnel, wherever he or she may be. Bring to their hearts a feeling of satisfaction in their service and a sense of accomplishment in their duty. Uplift their hearts in the absence from families and loved ones. Uplift the spirits of their families who wonder and wait. Enter their lives and hearts with a strong sense of your mercy and love and faith, an obedience to your will, and a love of the peace for which they serve. Amen

President of the Country

I am not sure there is anyone in the world more important than our president, in service to this country, its people, and in influence throughout the world. The person in this position, Lord, needs an almighty strength, a strong sense of duty and responsibility, and a dedicated faith to doing what is godly and right and good. Uphold our president, Lord, with strength from above, along with wisdom and guidance from your mercy. Uplift our president in times of turmoil, threat and indecision. Grant safety to our president, guarding against those who would seek to destroy. May our president and the family be comforted with peacefulness from above. Our secular leaders must know they are also in your service, Lord. Amen

Governor of the State

The people of our state elected a leader to keep the peace and promote good living for our part of the world. Work in our governor to fulfill those obligations, keeping the welfare of our state in high regard, and at the same time making us useful and important to our nation, other states, and the whole world. There are unique things about us, special resources and places that we have, histories and opportunities here in our state, for which we are thankful and responsible. Guide our governor to make appropriate decisions and to give fair leadership. Amen

Elected Officials

We must have leaders to manage our political life, our governments on all levels, that peace and good order may be maintained for all citizens. Bless those we have elected, or appointed, with a strong sense of duty and responsibility for the large task they have. Give them insight into planning well, communicating well, and holding the people they serve closely in their hearts. Guard them from enmity, jealousy, selfishness and greed. When their labor seems to be in vain, Lord pick up their spirits and their enthusiasm, and restore their energy. Give to these leaders a happy satisfaction in their positions. Amen

Mail Delivery Person

It is so easy to take for granted and forget about the importance of little daily items like getting the mail, along with the persons who provide this service. Help me to remember, with gratitude, what the mail delivery people are doing day after day for all of us. We are not happy to see the junk, but we are all glad to get the good letters and checks. Keep the mail persons' attitudes centered on their service for the good of all their recipients. Their jobs can surely be drudgery and turn negative. I pray, Lord, especially for happiness in their hearts and joy in their jobs, that they can feel the importance of what they are doing. Also, keep them safe. Amen

Garbage Collector

A service that can seem so thankless is the picking up and hauling away of our mountains of garbage and waste. As I easily wheel my containers to the street, I pray for the strength, safety and wellbeing of those who must come and haul it all away. Give them satisfaction in knowing that they are doing an important service for residents and the whole area. Many of these people may not have wanted the job they have. In the heat or cold of the seasons, with the difficulty of much of the work, and the unpredictable abuse that may happen, Lord bring to these workers the needed blessings of peace and health and satisfaction. Amen

Maid

A service that many would not want is the cleaning and care of someone else's home. Lord, I am thankful for the maid service that I have, and I pray that they will feel satisfied in knowing my appreciation for doing good work. I pray for good health and happy living for my maid, as well as all others who are doing this necessary service. In a world where so many people do not want to take the more humble jobs of serving or taking care of others, grant to those servers an inspired dedication. Help them to be diligent and responsible. Amen

Banker and Financial Advisor

Having others to help me in doing what I cannot do for myself alone is a great blessing. With thankfulness I acknowledge financial advisors and the important work they do. Lord, give insight, training, and a responsible attitude to those entrusted with the assets of others. In particular, I think of those who serve me directly in managing my finances. Lead them and me to correct decisions for my welfare and the good of others. Let us be cheerful about this important aspect of life. Amen

Pastor

Give to pastors, who have assumed their high callings, strong shoulders and big hearts and stable minds to serve as your ambassadors, Lord. I know that what may look happy and easy is not always so happy and so easy in serving people. Uplift my pastor, and other pastors I know, with a spirit that passes human understanding. Bless them with patience, satisfaction and love. Let the benediction of "well done, faithful servant" be an ongoing comfort and hope in pastors' lives. Amen

Church Musician

Realizing that worship music is a big part of spiritual life, Lord, let the music-makers in church know the satisfaction and joy of their wonderful service to those attending. Help them to be dedicated to spreading divine experience and uplifting hearts. The roots of faith and spiritual life for many people are in religious music, so guide the musicians to feel that it is a very important place that they hold. Bless their labors and talents, Lord, for the good of all. Amen

Cook

Food is a great blessing for us, but much of it would not be enjoyed without the expertise of cooks, and that includes the wonderful at-home cooks in families as well as the professional cooks in many places. Thanks be to God for those who prepare recipes and cook meals. Lord, give the cooks a sense of accomplishment and the reward of satisfaction to know that their efforts are important and enjoyed. Guide those who plan and make meals so that healthy service to others is their goal and purpose. Give them insight and dedication and patience. *Buen Provecho*! Amen

Waitperson

Lord, a waitperson who is in sync with my mood, personality and desires is such a blessing, improving my eating and drinking experience, making it so much more joyful. On the other hand, a waitperson who disappoints me tends to make me wish I were not there. No matter what the situation, I pray for the waitperson to develop and sharpen the service skills needed to bring satisfaction to customers and to enjoy the work. Help the waitperson realize how important good personal service is to all people. Continue to let waitpersons reap the rewards, mentally and financially, of a job well done. I know the work is not easy, and I am thankful for the satisfaction and added pleasure of good service. Amen

Pilot

Putting thoughtfulness and not-taking-for-granted into my view, I commit the training and professional work of airplane pilots into your hands, Lord. They are human beings entrusted with the care and lives of many other human beings. Give pilots a sense of dedication and responsibility to fulfill their jobs with great care and caution. Let them be guided by their training and knowledge of safety rather than any customer or company pressures. I am thankful for these professionals, Lord. Give them the strength and knowledge of their importance and good service. Amen

Repairman

Those who repair things for me are lifesavers, doing what I cannot do myself. Thank you, Lord, for people with the skill and training and desire to help others by fixing things. Often it is a humble dedication, with frustrations of timing, differences of opinion, and trials-and-errors. Give repair people knowledge and patience necessary for their important work, and then give them joy in their service. Help me to understand how difficult repair jobs may be and to be positive about dealing with those doing this important work. Often it is the little things that matter a great deal. Amen

MEDICAL CARETAKERS

Doctor

Medical diagnoses and treatments are usually beyond me, so I rely upon doctors for their professional services. I am thankful for the training, skills and dedication of the doctor who sees me. Lord, you have guided me to my doctors, and I ask your guidance for their decisions and treatments. Let the doctor's advice be right for my health and let it accomplish long-term benefits for me. Especially with the pressures of their work, give the doctor ongoing energy, enthusiasm, clarity and knowledge in my care and the care of others. Help us to keep me healthy. Amen

Nurse

Nurses carry out the contacts and communication for health care, as well as the hands-on personal care that is often needed. Bless them, Lord, for their service and dedication, that they may know the fruits of their labors. Give them a caring, loving spirit to deal with their patients. Guide those of us who receive the care of nurses to be cordial, agreeable and thankful. Nurses have a high responsibility of service to others, so take care of them, Lord. Amen

Medical Office Clerk

Mostly behind the scenes, the medical clerks fulfill important duties in health care. Grant to them, Lord, whatever is necessary for them to keep doing their jobs well. Help them with their attitudes and skills, as well as the accuracy of their work. Keep me reminded, Lord, to be kind and cooperative with the clerks who often may not receive the attention and gratitude that they deserve. Amen

Laboratory Technician

A specialized vocation means training and keeping up with changes, as well as the diligent daily duties of the work. Guide the technicians so that mentally and physically they may continue their important jobs in ways that will satisfy the patients as well as the other medical personnel that are served. Help them with the routine as well as the challenges. Help them to be steadfast and to be gratified by the results of their service. Amen

Pharmacist

Keep pharmacists well-trained and accurate, Lord, in dispensing medications to so many people. May the good results of their work be an inspiration to them to continue their services. Help them to handle the internal pressure they must feel to be careful and accurate with the wellbeing of others, and forgive them for their mistakes. Continue to work in the hearts of people to continue to do this important job, and continue to make me aware and thankful for them. Amen

Therapist

I often do not think about the dedication it takes for therapists to patiently work therapeutically with people who have needs for their services. These are people giving their time and lives to help others to live better.....over and over again, sometimes for long periods of time. Give them patience with a positive attitude, Lord. Let them know the joy and satisfaction of being builders, repairers, transformers. Help them to get their own needs met for building along the way. Let my cooperation be a good incentive for my therapists. Amen

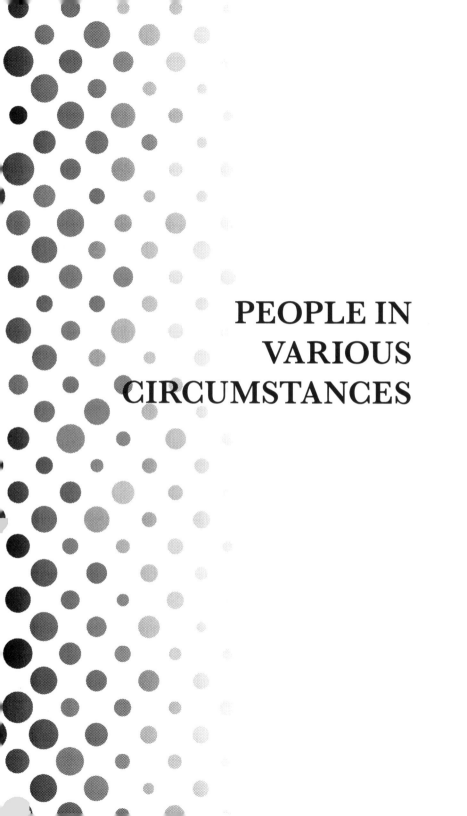

PEOPLE IN VARIOUS CIRCUMSTANCES

Happy with Spiritual Faith

It is so heartwarming to hear and know that someone I care about has the peace and the reassurance of spiritual faith. Life can be quite difficult, even devastating, and faith in a divine being, presence or power can be the strength needed to make it through the time. Thank you, God, for sending faith. Thank you for the confidence and joy that my loved one has. Continue to uplift and heal and bless and strengthen with good spiritual gifts for everyday living and for the troubled days that hit all of us. Put down evil with good, put out fear with faith, put up victory over defeat. Amen

Without Spiritual Faith

Because I believe that spiritual faith is so important, because I believe that living with your love in life and heart is so necessary, I ask for the miracle of faith for this loved one who has no faith. I want to believe that what I hear from this person's lips is not the truth of the heart. I want to hope that there is just some temporary glitch in full acceptance of your grace. I wish I could give faith to someone else as a gift. But this is my hoping, wishing, and maybe denying, and the acceptance by faith is really in your power, Lord. Our lives are in your hands. Use me as an influence, if it is your will. Bring the power of your Spirit into the heart of this person, along with a spiritual faith. There are many levels, many differences, many ways, many expressions – I am not one to judge. I just know that you love everyone and you want everyone. Let it be, Lord. Amen

Happy to Be at Work

Thank you God that this person likes to be at work. Some consider a job to be a necessary evil, and that is sad. Work is necessary, so what a blessing it is when a person enjoys it and likes to see the outcomes of labor. Keep this person in a good and happy spirit about work, Lord, even when it may be a difficult time, when there are dangers, or when physical health is reduced. Do not allow the rush of life to overtake a positive attitude. May there always be a job that is satisfying and pleasing for this person. Amen

Unhappy to Be at Work

The drudgery of having to do a job that is not pleasant or satisfying is a big burden for this person, Lord, and I pray for your guidance and strength. A positive and cooperative reaction to the necessity of working can make a huge difference in a person's character, and life can be so much more meaningful if work is an acceptable and agreeable routine with a happy outcome. Work in the mind and heart of this person to bring about a change in work outlook; or if there is a better job somewhere else, implement the changes that should be made. We know your desire is for joyful living in this world for all. Amen

Happy to Be in the Rain

Of all kinds of weather, rain seems to have the potential for inspiring different feelings in people. I am thankful for someone who likes the rain and is happy to see it or be in it. Rain can make them feel calm, peaceful, satisfied, enthused, passionate, creative, or energetic. Lord, continue to bring those good positive feelings from the blessing of your rain which waters the earth. Let there be more people who will like the rain. Amen

Unhappy to Be in the Rain

Please bring some peace and positive feeling to someone who is made unhappy by rain. Help them to see the good benefits that all the earth receives from the watering of the rains, even overcoming the depression of troubles from too much rain. Sometimes persons are unhappy about too many things that they cannot control, including rain, and mental adjustments are in order. Lead these people to help and change, that they may be happier with all of life. Amen

Happy to Be Home

Keep someone who is happy about being home content and satisfied to be there. Help to avoid jealous comparisons and unattainable desires that would spoil good feelings about home. Lord, help to make changes and adjustments that are necessary or desired as time goes along, but keep people comfortable and joyful in having their home and being in it. Let there be a feeling of peace and togetherness for all who are in that home. Amen

Unhappy to Be Home

I regret the sadness of someone who is not happy in his or her home, and I pray for a transforming and lifting of spirits that can change the unhappiness. Everyone should have a place to call home where they can feel comfortable, safe and peaceful. Guide the person who does not now have a happy home place into finding a home situation that will give blessings to enjoy. Whatever it takes, Lord, I know you can make the change, and people also can be changed. Amen

Happy on a Birthday

No matter what age we are talking about, there are persons who are happy that they get to celebrate another birthday, and I am thankful with them. I am thankful for that spirit that enjoys time and life, even when troubles and obstacles might come along with the years. Keep them joyful about a birthday, Lord, and keep them joyful about life. Let your blessings be evident, and help people always to see that they far outnumber the evils that threaten and afflict all of us. Amen

Unhappy on a Birthday

Someone who lets unhappiness rule the days of living will also be unhappy about a birthday, because it reminds that person of the troubles and trials of another year. I pray for a change of heart for that person. Give guidance, Lord, to some kind of help, some therapy or adjustment. Open the mind to realize negativity and unhappiness, and then grant the willingness to take action on seeking and making a change. Let the sound of "happy birthday" be a real goal. Amen

Happy to Be Going

A person who is going – moving, traveling, changing – can certainly be happy about it, and I ask your blessing and safety for that person, Lord. Help her or him to keep a happy heart in whatever activities or adjustments may be necessary, because if one is happy in doing something, that is a big step toward success and satisfaction. Whatever the reason for going, help to make the situation acceptable to all involved and keep hearts motivated by love and divine guidance. Amen

Unhappy to Be Going

I ask your uplifting power and divine guidance, Lord, for someone who is unhappy to have to be going, whether it is a move or change, temporary or permanent. Bring that person to see that your ways are not our ways, and that your divine presence is there to bring faith and peace wherever we are. Enlighten persons to put trust in you for all things. Give them a peaceful acceptance of things that we cannot control or change, and an optimistic outlook for all days. Amen.

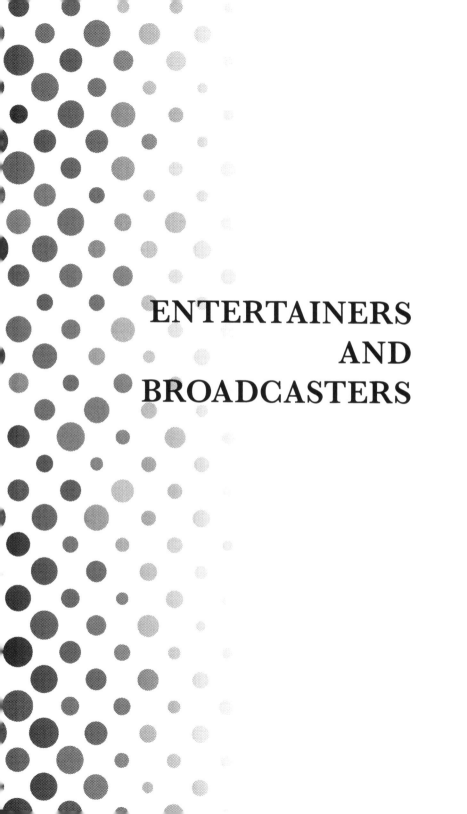

ENTERTAINERS AND BROADCASTERS

Reporters

So many reporters are attacked these days, some rightfully because of their "fake news" and others unjustly. Give the virtues of dedication, purpose and honesty to reporters, Lord, that they may present a dignified and moral profession to the public. Help those who need to make changes adjust their thinking and reporting to be fair and correct. Lift the spirits of those who are wrongly accused so that they may continue the good work they are doing. Bring peacefulness to the conflicts between reporters and their superiors, fair communication with politicians, and mutual appreciation with listeners and readers. Amen

Actors and Actresses

I admire the talent and hard work of those who perform in live theater, on television or in movies, or in any venue to entertain others. Give them satisfaction to know that their audiences realize it is no easy job to bring many different messages, and to instill laughter or tears or thinking. I ask strength and patience for entertainers. Let them reap rewards of joy in their hearts, without much regard to the physical and financial rewards that we know often come to them. May they labor to fulfill their life purposes and be blessed by the warm admiration of their fans. Amen

Musicians

Some musicians have the natural gift and some must work diligently to play, but I am thankful for all of those who are giving music to us. I do not like all music, but someone does, so it is all a blessing. Continue to inspire musicians to learn, practice and perform so that the labors of their profession may be well-received and enjoyed. Give them joy and satisfaction to know people are wanting to hear them. When they are tired and played out, Lord lift them up with more strength and dedication. Give them the notes so that we may get the messages. Amen

Sports Players

For many professional athletes, especially those in the top of the sports hierarchy, it has become more like an acting career, but the choice to be an athlete still comes with many risks, personal injuries and the need for hard work. Lift up athletes with courage and positive goals, and sustain them in safety and success. Help those who seem to be weakening get revitalized and strengthened for more winning. When athletes are losing, help them not to feel personally defeated, but enable them to see the big picture of a competitive career that will always have wins and losses. Keep greed, selfishness and animosity out of the picture. Amen

Writers

Behind many entertainers, reporters and performers are the writers who actually produce the material, so our prayers are important for those who do the creative writing work behind the scenes. Continue to provide training and inspiration for those who are writing for the success of public presentations. Give them the reward of satisfaction and joy when their work has culminated in many favorable reviews and reports. Motivate them to keep going when their work has not produced what they hoped. Amen

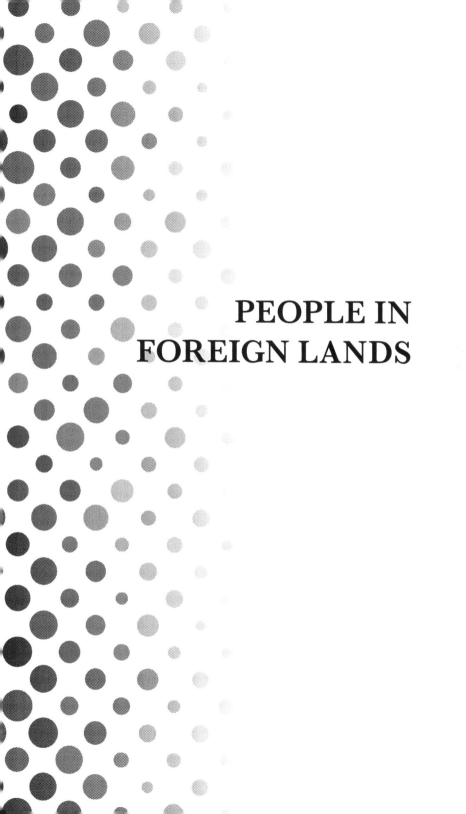

PEOPLE IN FOREIGN LANDS

People Starving

As I watch people send back plates half full of food, as I sit here not able to eat all of mine, as I see the heaps of wasted food in the alleys, I think about the many people who do not have enough to eat, and I am sorry, Lord. I am sorry for my own waste and that of so many others. Help us figure out how to better distribute available food. Open up ways for the hungry of the world to get enough to eat. Change the hearts of people who have power and access to distribute food to the starving millions. Work in the lives of hungry brothers and sisters so they may get food through their own work or from others. Food is a bare necessity, Lord, that the world has been blessed to produce. Direct people on every side to solve the tragedy of starvation wherever it is. Amen

People Ravaged by Warfare

Warfare has been a part of human existence throughout the ages, although many of us have not actually had to live in the midst of it. Thinking of those who are in war now, either active participants or caught in the turmoil, I pray, Lord, for their protection and wisdom. The majority of them do not want to be in a war, regardless of their allegiances. Help them to make decisions that will be good for safety and for the ending of the warfare. Guide leaders to strive for ending wars and the destruction that naturally occurs. Grant victories to those who will work for your will and your peace for all peoples. Amen

Those Who Have No Opportunity

The future is the most important part of hope and security for all people, and opportunities are the sparks of life for the future. Lord, many in the world cannot see any opportunities for their lives, and I pray that they may be given some insight to see possibilities. According to Your will, grant to people some chances for learning, for changing, for developing, for moving, for earning, for security, for happiness. Help them to see what may already be there for them, or create some opportunities for their futures. Inspire them to trust in divine intervention with mercy and love. Amen

People Who Are Not Free

Many of us take freedom for granted, but people in the world who are not free know the heavy burdens of slavery, entrapment, inferiority and restriction. It is for them I pray, that their burdens may be lifted. Maybe by small steps or maybe by a powerful swoop, may trapped people gain freedom. Grant to them the hearts and the attitudes to be free. Help people to learn how and when and where they can grasp freedom and be released from their disenfranchisement. Amen

Those Hurt by Tragedy

Natural disasters, human tragedies, and political disasters afflict large numbers of people all over the world. With today's communication, we hear about them regularly. I reach out in prayer for those afflicted by tragedies. Comfort those mourning losses of their loved ones, homes, and possessions. Wipe tears away with some signs of hope. Help them to make adjustments and achieve peace. Let resources flow from near and far to help these people in their time of great need. The questions of why this tragedy happened are always asked, and I pray that people may accept that we do not have the answer, except to say that evil leaves ugly destruction in its path throughout the world. Grant assurance of peace, hope and divine victory, Lord. Amen

Someone Struggling with a Burden

Because it is difficult to struggle alone with any burden, I ask your guidance and presence in the hard time through which this person is going. Physical burden, mental burden, social burden, financial burden, relationship burden, employment burden – they all are disheartening and consuming. If a decision needs to be made, Lord grant guidance. If action needs to be taken, Lord empower. If a change needs to be made, Lord prepare and assist. Help to lift this burden and make life satisfying and peaceful. Amen

Young People Who Want to Improve

There are young people in the world who have knowledge and motivation to improve their lives in different ways, but they are not able to move forward with their goals. Lord, I pray for your Spirit to open doors for young people so that they may achieve their dreams and ideas. To have the inner desire and attitude to go forward and become successful is a great blessing, but there must be an opening to education, development or position in which to achieve the goals. Please do not let these young people become disillusioned or harmed by lack of opportunity, but enable them to experience and accomplish. Amen

Children with Uncertainty

Some little children in the world, through no fault of their own, do not know where their next food will come from, or where they can sleep tonight, or how they can get help if they are sick. The world has resources, but distributing the necessities of life to everyone still seems to be beyond possibility. I pray for the poor children, Lord, who are living with such uncertainty. Life can be very difficult, but it seems too sad that just because of where or how they were born, some have to struggle to even keep living at a young age. Lift up the children, Lord, and help them to live. Grant the necessities for them to grow and mature so that they may have a chance to become adults and provide for themselves. Amen

Government Leaders

The leaders of the world have come to power in many different ways, which we may or may not find acceptable. But they have worldly powers and are in control, Lord, inasmuch as you allow, so I pray that you will use them for the good of your world and your people. Give leaders the hearts and minds that will cause them not to use their positions and powers for their selfish goals, which seems so prevalent, but rather to work for the building up of their countries and the entire world in peaceful ways. Put down and defeat evil wherever it is. Raise up world leaders who are capable, trustworthy and cooperative. Let your kingdom come throughout the world, Lord. Amen

Teachers

I thank God for teachers, wherever they are in the world. The training, abilities and dedication that are necessary to help others learn are commendable in this profession which is so valuable to the welfare of all the world. Continue to inspire teachers to use their experience and position to develop the minds and bodies of all students. Give teachers patience and understanding, so that they can be important to the lives of many different people. Help teachers to continue learning so that they can teach. Give them the insight to help students improve according to their individual needs and desires. Grant teachers a wonderful satisfaction in their life work. Amen

I Said a Prayer for You Today

I said a prayer for you today
and know God must have heard --
I felt the answer in my heart
although He spoke no word.....

I asked for happiness for you
in all things great and small,
but it was for His loving care
I prayed the most of all.

Author Unknown
(courtesy of Thad and Charlie)

About the Author

Roy Kenneth Bohrer was born and raised in the south suburbs of the Twin Cities, St. Paul and Minneapolis, Minnesota. He attended St. Olaf College, Northfield, Minnesota, received his bachelor of arts degree from the University of Minnesota, Minneapolis, and his master of divinity degree from Concordia Seminary, Springfield, Illinois.

Roy moved to Austin, Texas to serve as pastor of Christ Lutheran Church and still resides there now in retirement. In Austin he was involved in many community outreach programs, including youth, families and particularly the needs of senior citizens. After serving as a pastor, he was the executive director of several nonprofit professional associations, where he continued his interests in helping people to communicate, achieve and work together.

Prayerthink is born out of a lifetime of listening to, helping, and influencing many people from many different backgrounds, ages and circumstances. The idea of *prayerthink* comes from years of praying and the encouragement of friends. People are people. Human interaction is human interaction. Hearts are hearts. Needs are needs. Help is help.

Since retirement, Roy has had more time to pursue interests in travel, people and places. A prayer book he previously wrote and published, *When I Am Older, I Will Pray More,* is particularly aimed for the senior years.

Printed in the United States
By Bookmasters